I0820691

RICHARD NIXON

PIVOTAL PRESIDENTS
PROFILES IN LEADERSHIP

RICHARD NIXON

Edited by Julia Chandler

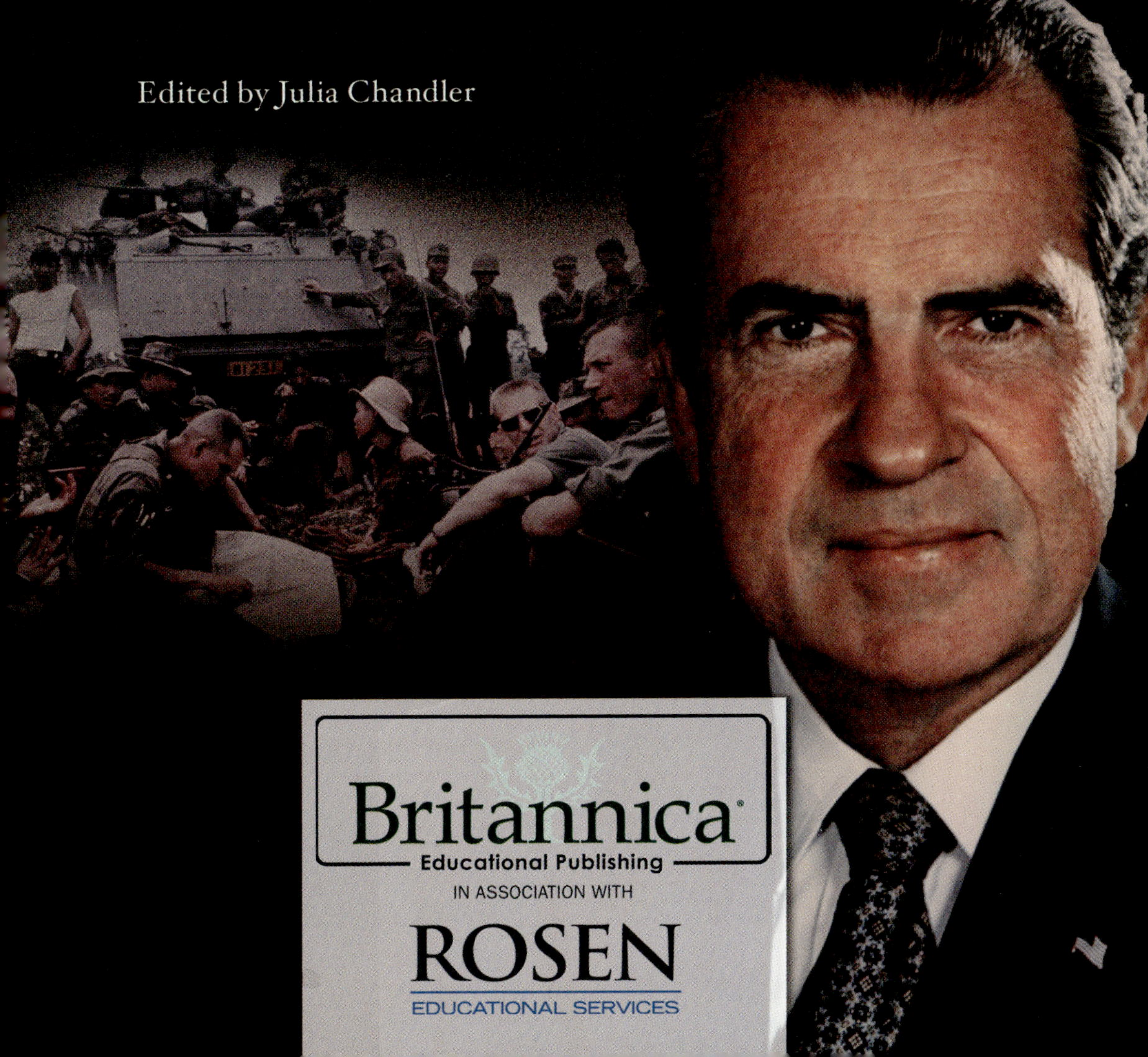

Britannica® Educational Publishing

IN ASSOCIATION WITH

ROSEN EDUCATIONAL SERVICES

Published in 2017 by Britannica Educational Publishing (a trademark of Encyclopædia Britannica, Inc.) in association with The Rosen Publishing Group, Inc.
29 East 21st Street, New York, NY 10010

Distributed exclusively by Rosen Publishing.
To see additional Britannica Educational Publishing titles, go to rosenpublishing.com.

First Edition

Britannica Educational Publishing
J.E. Luebering: Executive Director, Core Editorial
Anthony L. Green: Editor, Compton's by Britannica

Rosen Publishing
Julia Chandler: Editor
Nelson Sá: Art Director
Ellina Litmanovich: Designer
Cindy Reiman: Photography Manager
Bruce Donnola: Photo Researcher

Library of Congress Cataloging-in-Publication Data

Names: Chandler, Julia, 1988- editor.
Title: Richard Nixon / edited by Julia Chandler.
Description: First edition. | New York : Britannica Educational Publishing in association with Rosen Educational Services, 2017. | Series: Pivotal presidents: profiles in leadership | Includes bibliographical references and index. | Audience: Grades 7-12.
Identifiers: LCCN 2015050690 | ISBN 9781680485288 (library bound : alk. paper)
Subjects: LCSH: Nixon, Richard M. (Richard Milhous), 1913-1994. | Presidents--United States—Biography. | United States--Politics and government--1969-1974.
Classification: LCC E856 .R55 2016 | DDC 973.924092--dc23
LC record available at http://lccn.loc.gov/2015050690

Manufactured in China.

Photo credits: Cover, pp. 3 (portrait), 6 The White House/Archive Photos/Getty Images; cover, p. 3 (background) Hulton Archive/Archive Photos/Getty Images; cover, pp. 1, 3 (flag) © iStockphoto.com/spxChrome; p. 11 Popperfoto/Getty Images; p. 17, 29, 41, 51, 54, 59, 66 © AP Images; p. 18 Fox Photos/Hulton Archive/Getty Images; pp. 19, 24 Everett Collection Historical/Alamy Stock Photo; p. 21 MPI/Archive Photos/Getty Images; p. 27 George Silk/The LIFE Picture Collection/Getty Images; p. 31 © TopFoto/The Image Works; p. 32 Ralph Crane/The LIFE Picture Collection/Getty Images; p. 35 Oliver F. Atkin/White House Photo/Nixon Presidential Library and Museum/NARA; p. 39 Daily Express/Archive Photos/Getty Images; p. 44 Rolls Press/Popperfoto/Getty Images; p. 45 AFP/Getty Images; p. 47 © George W. Gardner/The Image Works; p. 57 The Washington Post/Getty Images; p. 62 Hulton Archive/Getty Images; p. 64 Album/SuperStock; p. 68 Gabriel Bouys/AFP/Getty Images; interior pages flag Fedorov Oleksiy/Shutterstock.com.

Table of Contents

INTRODUCTION

Nixon's presidency was cut short when the Watergate scandal forced him to resign.

In 1968, in a political comeback unprecedented in American history, Richard Nixon was elected the 37th president of the United States. Midway through his second term, however, his presidency came to a crushing halt. Facing a growing scandal and the prospect of impeachment, he became the first president to resign from office.

Nixon's 1968 victory followed two major political defeats. In his first bid for the presidency in 1960, the Democratic candidate, John F. Kennedy, narrowly defeated him. Two years later he lost his campaign for the governorship of his home state of California. He then temporarily retired from politics to practice law.

Before the election of 1960, Nixon's political career had been a series of unbroken successes. He was elected to the United States Congress in 1946 and entered the United States Senate as its youngest member in 1951. Two years later, at 39, he became the nation's second youngest vice president and served two terms under Republican Dwight D. Eisenhower.

Nominated for president again in 1968, Nixon won 301 electoral votes to defeat Vice President Hubert H. Humphrey. He spent much of his first term focusing on foreign policy. Through negotiations led by National Security Adviser Henry Kissinger and North Vietnamese Foreign Minister Le Duc Tho, U.S. involvement in the Vietnam War at last came to an end in early 1973. Meanwhile, Nixon reestablished diplomatic relations between the United States and China, which had halted after communists took control of China 21 years earlier. He was the first sitting president to visit China. In domestic policy, he reformed welfare policy, instituted the first affirmative action program, and battled inflation.

Renominated in 1972, Nixon polled a record 46 million popular votes and won 49 states. George McGovern, the Democratic candidate, received only 17 electoral votes. It was a landslide victory for Nixon. Yet by 1974 his impeachment seemed inevitable as a result of political scandals involving his staff.

During his reelection campaign, five burglars hired by the Committee to Reelect the President were arrested at the Democratic National Committee headquarters in the Watergate office-apartment-hotel complex in Washington, D.C. As the investigation continued, the Nixon Administration tried to cover up its connection to the burglary. In the summer of 1973 it was revealed that Nixon had taped conversations in the Oval Office. These tapes were then subpoenaed, but the president released only some of them.

The growing allegations against him led the House of Representatives to recommend three articles of impeachment charging Nixon with obstruction of justice, abuse of power, and failure to comply with congressional subpoenas. On August 5, 1974, Nixon finally released transcripts of three tapes that clearly implicated him in the cover-up. With this evidence, Nixon's impeachment by the House, and then conviction by the Senate, was almost assured. Rather than be forced from office, he resigned three days later, thus bringing an ignominious end to his political career.

Chapter 1

Early Life and Career

Richard Milhous Nixon was born in Yorba Linda, a farming village in Orange County, California, on January 9, 1913. He was the second of five sons of Francis (Frank) Anthony Nixon and Hannah Milhous Nixon.

Family History

Frank Nixon came from a Scots-Irish farming family. He was a descendant of James Nixon, who emigrated from Ireland to settle in Delaware in 1753. One member of the Nixon family served in the American Revolution. Another was killed in the battle of Gettysburg in the American Civil War.

Richard's father, who was born near McArthur, Ohio, had to go to work after

Young Richard Nixon *(right)* with his parents and brothers Harold *(left)* and Francis Donald, 1916.

having had only about six years of school. His last job in Ohio was as a streetcar motorman. One winter day his feet were frostbitten in the car, and he decided to move to a warmer climate. In Whittier, California, he took a job running a trolley.

Whittier was founded in 1887 as a Quaker settlement and named for the Quaker poet John Greenleaf Whittier. Here Frank Nixon met Hannah Milhous, his future wife. Hannah was one of nine children of Franklin Milhous, whose ancestors had emigrated from Germany to England and then to Ireland. Quakers in search of religious freedom, they came to Pennsylvania in 1729. When Hannah Milhous was born, her parents lived near Butlerville, Indiana. They moved to California in 1897.

Frank and Hannah met at a Quaker meetinghouse party in February 1908. Four months later they were married. Frank, who had been reared as a Methodist, became a Quaker. Their first son, Harold, was born in 1909.

Childhood in Yorba Linda and Whittier

The year before Richard was born, his father bought land in Yorba Linda. Here he built a house and started a lemon grove. Richard's brothers Francis Donald and Arthur were also born in Yorba Linda. The citrus-fruit venture proved unsuccessful, and after ten years' struggle the family returned to Whittier. There the last of the Nixon children, Edward, was born in 1930.

In Whittier, Frank Nixon set up a gas station, where he also began to sell a few groceries. Later he bought an old Quaker meetinghouse, which he moved next to the station to serve as a combination market and home. The business was a family enterprise. As soon as the boys were old enough, they helped in the store and in the station. Here young Richard learned his first lessons in dealing with the public. "I sold gas and delivered groceries and met a lot of people. I think this was invaluable as a start on a public career," Nixon said later.

Richard's mother, a devout Quaker, was patient, kind, and conscientious. His father was a rather severe man whose chief interest was politics. Frank Nixon's love of debate turned the market into a neighborhood club. At an age when most children are reading fairy tales, young Richard took an interest in politics and began reading the newspapers. He also absorbed his father's fondness for debate. While the boy was still in grammar school, his father helped him prepare his first public debate: "Resolved: It is more economical to rent a house than to own one."

Much of the Nixons' life centered upon religious activities. They went to the Quaker meetinghouse three times on Sunday and also attended Wednesday services. The boy, who had begun piano lessons at age seven, also played the church organ. One of the highlights of the year for the Nixon children was the Christmas reunion at Grandmother Milhous' home in Whittier. Richard was her favorite grandchild.

The Nixon family had its share of tragedy. Arthur, the second youngest boy, died when he was seven. When Richard was in high school, his older brother, Harold, contracted tuberculosis. In an effort to better Harold's health, his mother took him to Arizona for two years; however, he died in 1933.

While Hannah Nixon was away, Richard and his brother Francis Donald helped their father run the household and business. Richard was in charge of fruits and vegetables. Every morning he got up at 4:00 AM, drove 12 miles (19 km) to the produce market, and arranged the counter before school.

Nixon's Quakerism

Quakers belong to the Religious Society of Friends, a Christian denomination founded by George Fox in England in 1652. They have no ritual, sacraments, or ordained clergy. They appoint elders and overseers to serve at each meeting. Men and women who have received a "gift" are called recorded ministers. Meetings for worship are characterized by patient silence in which members wait for inspiration to speak as the "Inward Light"—the direct inner awareness of God—moves them.

Quakers oppose war because they feel that it causes spiritual damage through hatred. Most Quakers therefore refuse to perform military service and are excused as conscientious objectors. However, individuals follow their own convictions. Nixon, for example, chose to join the Navy during World War II.

Nixon's commitment to his Quaker roots was often inconsistent. On the one hand, his pacifist upbringing may have inspired his efforts as president to end the Vietnam War and establish more peaceful relations with China and the Soviet Union. As he stated in his first inaugural address, "The greatest honor history can bestow is the title of peacemaker."

On the other hand, Nixon may have distorted the Quaker belief that individuals have their own personal relationship with God to justify doing whatever he wanted as president. Journalist David Frost interviewed Nixon in 1977 and asked him about illegal wiretappings and break-ins that he had approved as president. Nixon responded, "When the president does it, that means it is not illegal." He clarified that the president cannot "run amok"

continued on the next page

continued from the previous page

because he must answer to the electorate and Congress. However, this statement still reveals that Nixon believed his powers as president had few limits, which may explain why he thought he would get away with covering up the Watergate scandal that led to his resignation.

COLLEGE AND LAW CAREER

At 17 Richard entered Whittier College, a Quaker institution that his mother had attended. In his first year he was elected president of his class and of a new fraternity, the Orthogonians. As a sophomore he represented Whittier in more than 50 debates, winning most of them. He became president of the student body during his senior year. He was also active in dramatics. In small groups he was reserved, but he lost his shyness when he faced a crowd. His major subject, history, was easy for him, but he had to work hard at science and mathematics. Nevertheless, he was second in his class when he graduated in 1934.

Nixon was a backup lineman on the football team at Whittier College.

Richard's ambition was to become a lawyer, but his brother's long illness had exhausted the family's savings. However, his good college record and the recommendations of his teachers enabled him to win a scholarship to Duke University, in Durham, North Carolina.

In Durham Nixon shared a $25-a-semester apartment with three other students. To help pay his living expenses, he worked in the college library. His classmates called him "Nix" or "Gloomy Gus" because of his tendency to brood. At Duke his leadership was soon recognized. He was elected president of the student body and in his final year became president of the Duke Bar Association. In June 1937 he graduated third in his class.

Five months later Nixon was admitted to the California bar. He joined the firm of

Nixon at the law offices of Bewley, Knoop, and Nixon, c. 1945.

Wingert and Bewley in Whittier. A short time after that it became Bewley, Knoop, and Nixon.

Marriage and Military Life

In the Whittier little theater group Nixon met "Pat" Ryan, a new teacher at the town

Richard and Pat Nixon pose with their marriage license.

high school. On June 21, 1940, two years after their first meeting, they were married.

Thelma Catherine Patricia Ryan was born on March 16, 1912, in Ely, Nevada. Her father, a silver miner, nicknamed her Pat. When she was a year old, the family moved to a 10-acre (4-hectare) truck farm in California, where she grew up. She was 13 at the time of her mother's death and 17 when her father died.

After a year at Fullerton Junior College, Pat drove an elderly couple to New York City, intending to stay only briefly. Instead, in 1931–32 she worked in a New York hospital, first as a secretary, then as an X-ray technician. She used her savings to enter the University of Southern California. While in college she played bit parts in movies. She graduated in 1937 and began her teaching career. After the Nixons were married, Pat continued to teach. The couple would have two daughters: Patricia (called Tricia), born on February 21, 1946, and Julie, born on July 5, 1948.

A few weeks after the United States entered World War II, Nixon went to Washington, D.C. In January 1942 he took a job with the Office of Price Administration.

Nixon *(third from left)* during his Navy service in the Pacific.

Two months later he applied for a Navy commission, and in September 1942 he was commissioned a lieutenant, junior grade. During much of the war he served as an operations officer with the South Pacific Combat Air Transport Command, rising to the rank of lieutenant commander.

Chapter 2

Congress and Vice Presidency

After the war Nixon returned to the United States, where he was assigned to work on Navy contracts while awaiting discharge. He was working in Baltimore, Maryland, when he received a telephone call that changed his life. A Republican citizen's committee in Whittier was considering Nixon as a candidate for Congress in the 12th Congressional District. In December 1945 Nixon accepted the candidacy with the promise that he would "wage a fighting, rocking, socking campaign."

Jerry Voorhis, a Democrat who had represented the 12th District since 1936, was running for reelection. Earlier in his career Voorhis had been an active socialist. He had become more conservative over the years and was now an outspoken opponent of communism. Despite Voorhis's anticommunist stand, the Los Angeles chapter of the left-wing Political Action Committee (PAC) endorsed him, apparently without his knowledge or approval.

The theme of Nixon's campaign was "a vote for Nixon is a vote against the communist-dominated PAC." The approach was successful. On November 5, 1946, Richard Nixon won his first political election.

The Hiss Case

As a freshman congressman, Nixon was assigned to the House Un-American Activities Committee. In this capacity he heard the testimony of Whittaker Chambers, a self-confessed former communist espionage agent, in August 1948. Chambers named Alger Hiss, a foreign policy adviser during Franklin D. Roosevelt's presidency, as an accomplice.

Hiss, a former State Department aide, asked for and obtained a hearing before the committee. He made a favorable impression, and the case would then have been dropped if not for Nixon, who urged investigation into Hiss's testimony on his relationship with Chambers.

Nixon *(right)* and investigator Robert Stripling examine the so-called "Pumpkin Papers," microfilm that showed Alger Hiss had shared secret State Department documents.

The committee let Nixon pursue the case behind closed doors. He brought Chambers and Hiss face to face. Chambers produced evidence proving that Hiss had passed State Department secrets to him. Among the exhibits were rolls of microfilm that Chambers had hidden in a pumpkin on his farm near Westminster, Maryland, as a precaution against theft. On December 15, 1948, a New York federal grand jury indicted Hiss for perjury. After two trials he was convicted, on January 21, 1950, and sentenced to five years in prison. The Hiss case made Nixon nationally famous.

While the case was still in the courts, Nixon decided to run for the Senate. In his 1950 senatorial campaign, he attacked the Harry S. Truman Administration and his opponent, Helen Gahagan Douglas, for being "soft" toward the communists. After his campaign distributed "pink sheets" comparing Douglas's voting record to that of Vito Marcantonio, a left-wing representative from New York, the *Independent Review*, a small Southern California newspaper, nicknamed him "Tricky Dick." The epithet later became a favorite among Nixon's opponents.

Nixon won the election by 680,000 votes, and at 38 he became the youngest member of the Senate. His Senate career was uneventful, and he was able to concentrate all his efforts on the upcoming 1952 presidential election.

The "Secret Fund"

Nixon did his work well. He hammered hard at three main issues—the war in Korea, communism in government, and the high cost of the Democratic Party's programs. At their 1952 national convention, the Republicans chose him as Eisenhower's running mate, to balance the ticket with a West Coast conservative.

Only a few days after the young senator's triumph, his political career seemed doomed. The *New York Post* printed a story headed "Secret Rich Men's Trust Fund Keeps Nixon in Style Far Beyond His Salary." The public was shocked. The Republicans were panic-stricken. Prominent members of the party urged Eisenhower to dump Nixon before it was too late.

There was really nothing secret about the fund. Nixon was a man of limited means, and when he won his Senate seat, a group of businessmen had publicly solicited funds to enable him to keep in touch with the voters in his home state while he served in the Senate. Nixon took his case directly to the people in a nationwide television address. He invited investigation of his finances and explained that no donor had asked for or received any favors. To demonstrate that he had not enriched himself in office, he listed his family's financial assets and liabilities in embarrassing detail, noting that his wife, Pat, unlike the wives of so many Democratic politicians, did not own a fur coat but only "a respectable Republican cloth coat."

Nixon's famous "Checkers speech" was broadcast on television on September 23, 1952.

The best-remembered part of his speech was his admission that an admirer had once sent the Nixons a small cocker spaniel named Checkers. "The kids love that dog, and I want to say right now that regardless of what they say, we're going to keep it," he declared.

The speech was a political triumph. Eisenhower asked Nixon to come to Wheeling, West Virginia, where he was campaigning. The president-to-be met his running mate at the airport with the words

"Dick, you're my boy." The Republicans won by a landslide.

Vice Presidency

The only duties listed for the vice president in the Constitution are to preside over the Senate and to vote if there is a tie. During his two terms as vice president, Nixon campaigned actively for Republican candidates but otherwise did not assume significant responsibilities. (Asked at a press conference to describe Nixon's contributions to his administration's policies, Eisenhower replied: "If you give me a week, I might think of one.")

However, Nixon regularly attended Cabinet meetings and meetings of the National Security Council. In the absence of the president he presided over these sessions. Thus Nixon was able to assume the president's duties when Eisenhower was incapacitated by illness—after a major heart attack in 1955, abdominal surgery in 1956, and a mild stroke in 1957. Eisenhower made an agreement with Nixon on the powers and responsibilities of the vice president in the event of presidential disability. The agreement was accepted by later administrations until the adoption of the Twenty-fifth Amendment to the U.S. Constitution in 1967.

During his eight years as vice president, Nixon made a series of goodwill tours that took him to every continent. In 1958 he faced rioting, rock-throwing mobs in Peru and Venezuela. In 1959 he engaged the Soviet Union's premier, Nikita Khrushchev, in an impromptu, profanity-filled debate in Moscow. It was known as the "kitchen debate" because it took place at the kitchen exhibit of the American National Exhibition in Sokolniki Park.

Nixon *(front right)* and Soviet Premier Nikita Khrushchev *(front left)* argued at the American National Exhibition in Moscow on July 24, 1959.

A "Political Obituary"

In 1960 the Republican Party chose its vice president to run for the nation's highest office. His running mate was Henry Cabot Lodge, Jr., a veteran of eight years as ambassador to the United Nations. Voters turned out in record numbers. When the 68 million votes were counted, John F. Kennedy had become the nation's first Roman Catholic president, and Richard Nixon had lost the presidential race by the narrow margin of about 100,000 votes. Nixon got 49.55 percent of the vote; Kennedy, 49.71 percent. Nixon carried 26 states for a total of 219 electoral votes. Kennedy carried 22 states and received 303 electoral votes.

The 1960 Presidential Debates

The highlight of the 1960 campaign was an unprecedented series of four television debates between Nixon and Kennedy. A provision of the Federal Communications Act had been suspended by Congress earlier in the year to permit the networks to broadcast the debates without having to provide equal time for candidates of minor parties. The debates were sometimes compared to the

From left, John F. Kennedy, moderator Frank McGee, and Nixon at the debate on October 8, 1960.

historic debates between Abraham Lincoln and Stephen A. Douglas when they were running for an Illinois Senate seat in 1858. However, the 1960 debates were more in the nature of joint press conferences, with reporters asking questions.

About 85–120 million Americans watched one or more of the debates, which provided voters with an opportunity to compare the two candidates. Although Nixon showed a mastery of the issues, it was generally agreed that Kennedy, with his relaxed and self-confident manner, as well as his good looks (in contrast to Nixon's "five o'clock shadow"), benefited more from the exchanges.

Nixon's supporters blamed his defeat on voting irregularities in both Texas and Illinois. Some prominent Republicans—including Eisenhower—even urged Nixon to contest the results. He chose not to, however, declaring:

> *I could think of no worse example for nations abroad, who for the first time were trying to put free electoral procedures into effect, than that of the United States wrangling over the results of our presidential election, and even suggesting that the presidency itself could be stolen by thievery at the ballot box.*

In front of a board showing election returns, Nixon conceded the 1960 election at the Ambassador Hotel in Los Angeles.

Nixon's supporters and critics alike, both then and later, praised him for the dignity and unselfishness with which he handled defeat and the suspicion that vote fraud had cost him the presidency.

Other reasons given for the defeat were his poor appearance in a series of television debates with Kennedy; his unwillingness, because of the president's ill health, to let Eisenhower conduct a full-fledged campaign for him; and his refusal to permit any discussion of religion in the campaign. Also, the Republicans lacked the support of organized labor, and their social-welfare program was no match for that of the Democrats. Whatever the reasons, Nixon had lost an election for the first time, and he seemed to be out of the political picture.

Two years later Nixon was the Republican candidate for governor in his native California. The incumbent, Edmund G. (Pat) Brown, defeated him. In his "last press conference," Nixon attacked the news media and announced his retirement from politics.

Nixon left California for New York, where he entered a substantial law practice. His image as a "loser" in politics seemed complete. A television network even ran a documentary entitled *The Political Obituary of Richard M. Nixon.*

CHAPTER 3

Presidency

In 1964 Nixon made no move toward the presidency. Instead he traveled some 50,000 miles (80,000 km) and visited 36 states on behalf of Barry M. Goldwater, the conservative Republican candidate. Goldwater's overwhelming defeat was portrayed as a disaster for the Republican Party, which was already torn by disagreement between its conservative and its liberal members. The setback, however, was only temporary.

Nixon, stepping in as a unifying force, began to campaign for Republican candidates around the country. In 1966 his efforts helped the Republicans gain 47 House seats and 3 additional seats in the Senate. By the time the 1968 presidential campaign got under way, Republicans all over the country owed Nixon support.

VICTORY IN 1968

In the 1968 primary elections, Nixon began to cast off the "loser" image. He won the Republican nomination for president by putting together a coalition that included Southern conservatives led by Senator Strom Thurmond of South Carolina. In exchange for Southern support, Nixon promised to appoint "strict constructionists" to the federal judiciary,

Nixon during a campaign stop in 1968, saluting the crowd with his iconic "V is for Victory" gesture.

to name a Southerner to the Supreme Court, and to oppose court-ordered busing. For his running mate he chose Spiro T. Agnew, the governor of Maryland, a man little known outside his own state. Agnew was a compromise choice who was acceptable to Republicans from both the North and the South.

Throughout the election campaign, Nixon deplored the growing rate of crime in the streets, called attention to the high cost and the limitations of the Democrats' welfare programs, and denounced their inaction against inflation. In promising an honorable peace in Vietnam, Nixon claimed he had a "secret plan" to end the war. His Democratic opponent, Hubert H. Humphrey, was Lyndon B. Johnson's vice president and therefore associated with the president's unpopular Vietnam policies. Johnson halted the bombing of North Vietnam on October 31, less than one week before the election, in preparation for direct negotiations to end the war. Had he taken this step earlier, Humphrey might have won the election, as polls showed him gaining rapidly on Nixon in the final days of the campaign.

Nixon won the election by a narrow margin, 31.7 million popular votes to Humphrey's nearly 30.9 million; the electoral vote was 301 to 191.

About a month before Nixon's inauguration on January 20, 1969, his younger daughter, Julie, was married to David Eisenhower, the grandson of former President Eisenhower.

Foreign Policy

In his inaugural address, Nixon emphasized his determination to seek peace abroad, especially in Vietnam, and to bring about a reconciliation of the differences that divided the United States. He turned his attention primarily to foreign affairs. In February 1969 he visited Belgium, England, West Germany, Italy, and France in an effort to strengthen the North Atlantic Treaty Organization (NATO).

To assure noncommunist Asian nations of continued U.S. support, Nixon embarked in late July on a tour of the Philippines, Indonesia, Thailand, India, Pakistan, and South Vietnam. Nixon then visited Romania. He was the first American president to enter a Soviet-bloc nation since World War II.

Vietnam

Aiming to achieve "peace with honor" in the Vietnam War, Nixon gradually reduced the number of U.S. military personnel in

Vietnam. By autumn 1972 U.S. troop strength in Vietnam—which in April 1969 had reached a peak of 543,000 men—was 32,200 men. Under his policy of "Vietnamization," combat roles were transferred to South Vietnamese troops, who nevertheless remained heavily dependent on American supplies and air support. At the same time, however, Nixon resumed the bombing of North Vietnam (which had been suspended by President Johnson in October 1968) and expanded the air and ground war to neighboring Cambodia and Laos.

In the spring of 1970 U.S. and South Vietnamese forces attacked North Vietnamese sanctuaries in Cambodia, which prompted widespread protests in the United States. One of these demonstrations—at Kent State University on May 4, 1970—ended tragically when soldiers of the Ohio National Guard fired into a crowd of about 2,000 protesters, killing four and wounding nine. Early in 1972 the North Vietnamese mounted an offensive against the South, which had uneven success in defending itself. In a move to cut off military supplies to Hanoi, Nixon ordered the mining of North Vietnamese ports and the bombing of overland supply routes from China.

In January 1973 Le Duc Tho of North Vietnam *(left)* and Henry Kissinger of the United States signed a peace agreement in Paris that ended U.S. involvement in the Vietnam War.

After intensive negotiations between National Security Adviser Henry Kissinger and North Vietnamese Foreign Minister Le Duc Tho, the two sides reached an agreement in October 1972, and Kissinger announced, "Peace is at hand." But the South Vietnamese raised objections, and the agreement quickly broke down. An intensive 11-day bombing campaign of Hanoi and other North Vietnamese cities in late December (the "Christmas bombings") was followed by more negotiations, and a new agreement was finally reached in January 1973 and signed in Paris. It included an immediate cease-fire, the withdrawal of all American military personnel, the release of all prisoners of war, and an international force to keep the peace. For their work on the accord, Kissinger and Tho were awarded the 1973 Nobel Prize for Peace (though Tho declined the honor). In March Nixon welcomed home the last American ground troops and prisoners of war from Vietnam. American military involvement continued with bombing raids over Cambodia until mid-August.

China and the Soviet Union

Nixon's most significant achievement in foreign affairs may have been the establishment of direct relations with the People's Republic of China after a 21-year estrangement. After a long civil war, the People's Republic of China was proclaimed in 1949 under a communist government. The Nationalists fled to the island of Taiwan, off the southeastern Chinese coast, and established the Republic of China. Ever since, the United States had recognized the Republic of China as the legitimate government of all China.

Following a series of low-level diplomatic contacts in 1970 and the lifting of U.S. trade and travel restrictions the following year, officials

Richard and Pat Nixon tour the Great Wall during their visit to China in February 1972.

from the People's Republic of China indicated that they would welcome high-level discussions. Nixon sent his national security adviser, Henry Kissinger, to China for secret talks. The thaw in relations became apparent with the "ping-pong diplomacy" conducted by American and Chinese table-tennis teams in visits in 1971–72.

Nixon's visit to China in February–March 1972, the first by an American president while in office, concluded with the Shanghai Communiqué. In this brief, the United States formally recognized the "one-China" principle—that there is only one China, and that Taiwan is a part of China. In February 1973 it was revealed that the United States and the People's Republic of China would set up government liaison offices in Washington, D.C., and in Beijing. The United States did not officially switch its diplomatic recognition from Taiwan to the People's Republic of China until early 1979.

The rapprochement with China was undertaken in part to take advantage of the growing rift between the Chinese and the Soviets in the late 1960s. Thawing relations with China gave Nixon more leverage in his dealings with the Soviet Union. By 1971 the Soviets were more amenable to improved relations with the United States, and in May 1972 Nixon paid a state visit to Moscow to sign 10 formal agreements. The most important were the nuclear arms limitation treaties known as SALT I (based on the Strategic Arms Limitation Talks conducted between the United States and the Soviet Union beginning in 1969). In June 1973 Nixon hosted a visit from Leonid I. Brezhnev, general secretary of the Soviet Communist Party. The two leaders signed a friendship agreement. They also expanded scientific, technical, educational, and cultural exchanges and agreed to hold additional negotiations to limit nuclear arsenals.

The Middle East and Latin America

Nixon was less successful in the Middle East. His administration's comprehensive plan for peace, the Rogers Plan (named for Nixon's first secretary of state, William Rogers), was rejected by both Israel and the Soviet Union. War erupted in the Middle East in October 1973 when Syria and Egypt attacked Israel simultaneously. The war was known as the "Yom Kippur War" or the "Ramadan War" because it took place during those religious observances. Kissinger made back-and-forth visits between the Arab states and Israel (dubbed "shuttle

Israeli soldiers advance into Syria during the Yom Kippur War (or Ramadan War) of 1973.

diplomacy") to end the war. However, his efforts did little to improve U.S. relations with the Arabs.

Fearing communist revolution in Latin America, the Nixon Administration helped to undermine the coalition government of Chile's Marxist President Salvador Allende, elected in 1970. After Allende nationalized American-owned mining companies, the administration restricted Chile's access to international economic assistance and discouraged private investment. The United States also increased aid to the Chilean military, made secret contacts with anti-Allende police and military officials, and funneled millions of dollars in covert payments to Chilean opposition groups in 1970–73. In September 1973 Allende was overthrown in a military coup led by army commander in chief General Augusto Pinochet.

Chilean soldiers burn Marxist literature during the coup that overthrew President Salvador Allende in September 1973.

Domestic Policy

Despite expectations from some observers that Nixon would be a "do-nothing" president, his administration undertook a number of important reforms in welfare policy, civil rights, law enforcement, the environment, and other areas.

The Economy

Prior to 1973 the most important of Nixon's domestic problems was the economy. In order to reduce inflation, he initially tried to restrict federal spending. But beginning in 1971 his budget proposals contained deficits of several billion dollars, the largest in American history up to that time. In August 1971 Nixon announced his New Economic Policy in response to continuing inflation, increasing unemployment, and a deteriorating trade deficit. It included an 8 percent devaluation of the dollar, new surcharges on imports, and unprecedented peacetime controls on wages and prices. These policies produced temporary improvements in the economy by the end of 1972. However, once price and wage controls were lifted, inflation returned with

Marchers protest rising food prices in New York City in 1973.

a vengeance, reaching 8.8 percent in 1973 and 12.2 percent in 1974. In February 1973 Nixon announced his second devaluation of the dollar. In June he ordered a 60-day freeze on all retail and wholesale prices except for raw agricultural commodities. Price controls in some form were in effect until Congress let them expire on April 30, 1974.

Another economic problem was the energy crisis of 1973. U.S. demand for imported oil was rising rapidly, and the Organization of Petroleum Exporting Countries (OPEC) took advantage of the changing market, as well as the disruption of the latest Arab-Israeli war, to raise prices sharply, from about $3 to more than $12 per barrel.

The Nixon Administration instituted several measures to try to reduce Americans' oil consumption. The Emergency Highway Energy Conservation Act set speed limits on highways to 55 miles per hour (88 kph), a more fuel-efficient rate than higher speeds (this act was not repealed until 1995). Gas shortages meant long lines at stations. Some states instituted a policy where people could only fuel up their cars on odd days if their license plate ended in an odd number, and vice versa for even days and numbers.

WELFARE REFORM, CIVIL RIGHTS, AND OTHER PROGRAMS

Nixon proposed the Family Assistance Program (FAP) to provide working and nonworking poor families with a guaranteed annual income—though he preferred to call it a "negative income tax." Although the measure was defeated in the Senate, its failure helped to generate support for other legislation that incorporated similar ideas. Supplemental Security Income (SSI) provided a guaranteed income to the elderly, the blind, and the disabled. Congress also passed automatic cost-of-living adjustments (COLAs) for Social Security recipients and expanded and improved existing programs, such as food stamps and health insurance for low-income families.

In the area of civil rights, Nixon's administration instituted so-called "set aside" policies to reserve a certain percentage of jobs for minorities on federally funded construction projects. This was the first "affirmative action" program. Although Nixon opposed school busing and delayed taking action on desegregation until federal court orders forced his hand, he believed strongly in equality between the races. His administration drastically reduced the percentage of African American students attending all-black schools. In addition, funding for many federal civil rights agencies, in particular the Equal Employment Opportunity Commission (EEOC), was substantially increased while Nixon was in office.

In response to pressure from consumer and environmental groups, Nixon proposed legislation that created the Occupational Safety and Health Administration (OSHA) and the Environmental Protection Agency (EPA). His revenue-sharing program, called "New Federalism," provided state and local governments with billions of federal tax dollars to take over federal programs in urban development, education, manpower training, and law enforcement.

Earth Day and the EPA

In the late 1960s Americans became increasingly concerned about the environment. Sharing these concerns was U.S. Senator Gaylord Nelson of Wisconsin. A well-known advocate for the environment, Nelson wanted to bring Americans together on this issue by creating a national celebration of the Earth. He enlisted Denis Hayes, then a graduate student at Harvard University in Massachusetts, to help organize the event. The first Earth Day took place on April 22, 1970. More than 20

million people across the United States participated, many of them through events at schools, colleges, and universities.

The success of the first Earth Day helped gain support for a number of environmental laws in the United States. These included the Clean Air Act (1970), the Federal Environmental Pesticide Control Act (1972), the Clean Water Act (1972), and the Endangered Species Act (1973).

Later in 1970 President Nixon created the Environmental Protection Agency (EPA) to set and enforce national pollution-control standards. One of

continued on the next page

A senator and two Nixon Administration officials examine dead eagles during a hearing on environmental issues in 1971.

continued from the previous page

the EPA's early successes was an agreement with automobile manufacturers to install catalytic converters in cars, thereby reducing emissions of unburned hydrocarbons by 85 percent. The EPA's enforcement was in large part responsible for a decline of one-third to one-half in most air-pollution emissions in the United States from 1970 to 1990. Among other issues, the EPA works to control ocean dumping, unsafe drinking water, insecticides, and asbestos hazards in schools. The EPA also develops strategies to manage emissions of carbon dioxide and other greenhouse gases.

During his presidency, Nixon appointed four justices to the Supreme Court. Chief Justice Earl Warren had announced his retirement before Nixon's inauguration, but the Senate blocked President Lyndon B. Johnson's nomination of associate justice Abe Fortas, giving Nixon the opportunity to make a selection. The Senate approved his nominee, Warren E. Burger. Nixon's appointments for associate justice were Harry A. Blackmun (1970), William H. Rehnquist (1971), and Lewis F. Powell (1971).

CHAPTER 4

Watergate and Resignation

Renominated with Agnew in 1972, Nixon conducted his campaign for a second term by surrogate. While he seldom left his White House office, the vice president and other associates campaigned for him. He defeated his Democratic challenger, liberal Senator George S. McGovern, in one of the largest landslide victories in the history of American presidential elections: 46.7 million to 28.9 million in the popular vote and 520 to 17 in the electoral vote. Supporters interpreted his landslide victory as a mandate for his programs. Nevertheless, Nixon would soon be forced to resign in disgrace in the worst political scandal in U.S. history.

In fact, scandal plagued both the president and vice president in 1973. That summer Agnew was investigated in connection

Vice President Spiro T. Agnew *(center)* **leaves court after pleading no contest to income tax evasion.**

with accusations of extortion, bribery, and income-tax violations relating chiefly to his tenure as governor of Maryland. He resigned from office on October 10, 1973, and pled no contest in federal court on a felony charge of income tax evasion; he was sentenced to three years of probation and fined $10,000. Nixon chose Representative Gerald R. Ford of Michigan as Agnew's successor, and Congress confirmed him.

Reports circulated that year about Nixon's low tax payments in proportion to his income. In 1974 the Joint Committee on Internal Revenue Taxation and the Internal Revenue Service found that Nixon owed more than $400,000 in back taxes. However, an even bigger scandal was the ultimate downfall of his presidency.

The Watergate Break-In

The Watergate scandal stemmed from illegal activities by Nixon and his aides related to the burglary and wiretapping of the national headquarters of the Democratic Party at the Watergate office complex in Washington, D.C. Eventually it came to encompass allegations of other loosely related crimes committed both before and after the break-in.

The five men involved in the burglary, who were hired by the Republican Party's Committee to Reelect the President, were arrested and charged on June 17, 1972. In the days following the arrests, Nixon secretly directed the White House counsel, John Dean, to oversee a cover-up to conceal the administration's involvement. Nixon also obstructed the Federal Bureau of Investigation (FBI) in its inquiry and authorized secret cash payments to the Watergate burglars in an effort to prevent them from implicating the administration.

Several major newspapers investigated the possible involvement of the White House in the burglary. Leading the pack was *The Washington Post* and its two hungry newshounds, Carl Bernstein and Bob Woodward. Their stories were based largely on information from an unnamed source called "Deep Throat." The mysterious identity of Deep Throat became a news story in its own right and led to decades of speculation. W. Mark Felt, a top-ranking FBI official at the time of the

Bob Woodward *(left)* and Carl Bernstein in the newsroom of *The Washington Post* in 1973.

investigation, revealed himself as the informant in 2005.

The burglary did not have much impact on the 1972 election. The White House successfully framed Woodward and Bernstein's reporting as the obsession of a single "liberal" newspaper pursuing a vendetta against the president. Limited coverage in other newspapers and on television allowed Nixon to win handily.

Congressional Investigations

In February 1973 a special Senate committee—the Select Committee on Presidential Campaign Activities, chaired by Senator Sam Ervin—was established to look into the Watergate affair. In televised committee hearings, John Dean accused the president of involvement in the cover-up. Others testified to illegal activities by the administration and the campaign staff. Federal agencies reportedly harassed Nixon's perceived enemies (many of whose names appeared on an "enemies list" of prominent politicians, journalists, entertainers, academics, and others). A special White House investigative unit was known as the "plumbers" because they investigated news leaks.

As Senator Howard Baker of Tennessee, the vice chairman of the committee,

John Dean testifies before the Senate about Watergate on June 27, 1973.

eloquently put it, the key question in the scandal was "What did the president know and when did he know it?" Nothing, Nixon continuously maintained. However, in July the committee learned that in 1969 Nixon had installed a recording system in the White House and that all the president's conversations in the Oval Office had been recorded. Archibald Cox, the special prosecutor appointed to investigate the

Watergate affair, subpoenaed the tapes, but Nixon refused to comply, offering to provide summary transcripts instead. Cox rejected the offer.

Then, in a series of episodes that came to be known as the Saturday Night Massacre, Nixon ordered Attorney General Elliot Richardson to fire Cox, and Richardson resigned rather than comply. Nixon then fired Richardson's assistant, William Ruckelshaus, when he too refused to fire Cox. Cox was finally removed by Solicitor General Robert Bork, though a federal district court subsequently ruled the action illegal.

The "Smoking Gun"

Amid calls for his impeachment, Nixon agreed to the appointment of another special prosecutor, Leon Jaworski, and promised that he would not fire him without congressional consent. On October 23, Nixon released seven of the nine tapes requested by Cox, one of which contained a suspicious gap of 18 and a half minutes. Although damning, the tapes did not contain the "smoking gun" that would prove

Impeachment

Impeachment is a legal procedure in which a public official is indicted for, or accused of, misdeeds he or she is suspected of having committed. But instead of the case going to a regular jury trial, a legislative body conducts hearings to weigh evidence against the accused. According to Article II, section 4, of the U.S. Constitution, any federal officer may be impeached, including the president and vice president. At the federal level, the House of Representatives votes on each article of impeachment. If any one of the articles is approved by a simple majority, the accused is impeached, and the Senate then holds a trial. A conviction requires a vote in favor by at least two-thirds of the senators.

The impeachment process has rarely been employed, but there have been three famous cases involving presidents. Andrew Johnson and Bill Clinton were both impeached by the House. In Johnson's case, the charges were clearly political, a result of his quarrel with the Radical Republicans in Congress over the direction of Reconstruction. At his trial in the Senate in 1868, Johnson was acquitted by only one vote.

In 1998 the House of Representatives approved two articles of impeachment against Clinton, charging him with perjury and obstruction of justice in his effort to conceal his affair with White House intern Monica Lewinsky. Clinton also survived his Senate trial, with the senators finding him not guilty of perjury (by a vote of 55–45) and obstruction of justice (by a vote of 50–50).

Bill Clinton was acquitted in his Senate impeachment trial on February 12, 1999.

Nixon's case was different. As a result of the Watergate scandal, the Judiciary Committee of the House of Representatives voted three articles of impeachment against Nixon in July 1974. However, because he would likely be found guilty and removed from office, he resigned before impeachment proceedings could begin in the full House.

that the president himself ordered the break-in or attempted to obstruct justice. In a news conference on November 17, Nixon defended his record and declared, "I am not a crook."

Jaworski later subpoenaed 64 tapes that Nixon continued to withhold on grounds of "executive privilege." In July 1974 the Supreme Court ruled unanimously that Nixon's claims of executive privilege were invalid. By that time the House Judiciary Committee had already voted to recommend three articles of impeachment, relating to obstruction of justice, abuse of power, and failure to comply with congressional subpoenas. On August 5, in compliance with the Supreme Court's ruling, Nixon submitted transcripts of a conversation taped on June 23, 1972, in which he discussed a plan to use the Central Intelligence Agency to block the FBI's investigation of the Watergate break-in. The smoking gun had finally been found.

Faced with the near-certain prospect of impeachment by the House and conviction in the Senate, Nixon announced his resignation on the evening of August 8, 1974, effective at noon the next day. As he

Nixon delivers his resignation speech on August 8, 1974.

put it, he no longer had "a strong enough political base" with which to govern. Ford, who had been vice president for less than a year, was sworn in as president. Within a month, he granted Nixon a full pardon for all crimes he may have committed during his administration.

Aftermath

By the time of the pardon, many Americans had become convinced that Nixon was guilty of crimes and that Ford had pardoned him as quid pro quo for becoming president. The approval rating of the otherwise popular new president collapsed overnight.

This loss of faith in the new chief executive spoke to the extraordinary cynicism of Americans in the wake of Watergate. The scandal had dragged on for more than two years by that point; eventually, many of Nixon's closest aides went to jail. For the rest of the decade both popular and political culture were marked by paranoia and disillusionment.

Even in the early 21st century, the legacy of Watergate continued to haunt American politics. Watergate was so synonymous

In an unpopular decision, President Gerald Ford, Nixon's successor, pardoned Nixon on September 8, 1974, "for all offenses against the United States" that he had committed "or may have committed" while in office.

with scandal that it became common practice for the press to tack on a "gate" to other scandals, such as "Troopergate" or "Deflategate." The former president and then, after his death, his family spent a great deal of money on a legal campaign to prevent the entirety of his tapes from being released. That effort failed, and the entire taped record of the Nixon White House eventually became available to the public.

Conclusion

Nixon retired with his wife to the seclusion of his estate in San Clemente, California. He wrote *RN: The Memoirs of Richard Nixon* (1978) and several books on international affairs and American foreign policy, modestly rehabilitating his public reputation and earning a role as an elder statesman and foreign-policy expert. Nixon spent his last years campaigning for American political support and financial aid for Russia and the other former Soviet

In 2011 the Nixon Presidential Library and Museum opened a new, more balanced exhibit on Watergate to replace one that had downplayed the former president's role in the scandal.

republics. The Richard Nixon Library in Yorba Linda was dedicated in 1991.

Nixon died of a massive stroke in New York City in April 1994, 10 months after his wife's death from lung cancer. He was buried beside his wife at his birthplace.

If not for the Watergate scandal, Nixon likely would have been remembered as a strong president who ended the Vietnam War, opened a new era in foreign relations, and introduced programs such as affirmative action and "New Federalism" revenue sharing. Instead, he chose to abuse his power by attempting to cover up a criminal conspiracy, leaving him with a disgraceful legacy: the first (and so far only) president to resign his office before he could be impeached and removed by Congress.

Glossary

affirmative action An active effort to improve employment or educational opportunities for members of minority groups and women.

communism A political and economic system in which the major productive resources in a society—such as mines, factories, and farms—are owned by the public or the state.

conscientious objector A person who refuses to serve in the military because of moral or religious beliefs.

denounce To pronounce that a person or idea is wrong or blameworthy.

devaluation An official reduction in the exchange value of a currency by lowering its gold equivalency.

epithet A disparaging or abusive word or phrase.

estrangement Separation or severing of friendly relations.

executive privilege Exemption from legally enforced disclosure of communications within the executive branch of government when such disclosure would adversely affect that branch's functions and decision-making processes.

extortion The act of obtaining something, especially money or property, from an unwilling party through intimidation, force, or abuse of power.

ignominious Marked by disgrace or shame; dishonorable.

impeachment A legal procedure by which an elected official is accused of misconduct while in office.

incapacitated Made incapable; disabled.

indict To charge with a crime.

inflation A continuing rise in the general price level usually attributed to an increase in the volume of money and credit relative to available goods.

obstruct To hinder from passing, action, or operation.

perjury The crime of telling a lie under oath during a trial or other legal proceeding.

quid pro quo Something given or received in return for something else.

rapprochement The establishment of cordial relations.

subpoena A written order commanding someone to appear in court or to produce certain evidence, such as documents or recordings.

tuberculosis An infectious disease spread through coughing or sneezing that mainly affects the lungs. Other symptoms include fever, night sweats, and weight loss.

Vietnamization The act or process of transferring war responsibilities from U.S. to South Vietnamese hands during the Vietnam War.

For More Information

Environmental Protection Agency (EPA)
1200 Pennsylvania Avenue NW
Washington, DC 20460
(202) 272-0167
Website: http://www3.epa.gov
The formation of the EPA was one of several important environmental measures taken during Nixon's presidency. The EPA works to protect human health and the environment in areas such as air quality, chemical safety, water protection, and sustainability.

The Miller Center
P.O. Box 400406
Charlottesville, VA 22904
(434) 924-7236
Website: http://millercenter.org
The Miller Center, based at the University of Virginia, is a nonpartisan research facility

focused on the history of the U.S. presidency. One of the center's ongoing projects is to transcribe and interpret the secret White House recordings of presidents Franklin D. Roosevelt, Harry S. Truman, Dwight D. Eisenhower, John F. Kennedy, Lyndon B. Johnson, and Richard Nixon.

National Museum of American History
14th Street and Constitution Avenue NW
Washington, DC 20001
(202) 633-1000
Website: http://americanhistory.si.edu/presidency
One of the ongoing exhibits at the Smithsonian's National Museum of American History is entitled "The American Presidency: A Glorious Burden," which examines how American presidents have impacted history.

Nixon Presidential Library and Museum
18001 Yorba Linda Boulevard
Yorba Linda, CA
(714) 983-9120
Website: http://www.nixonlibrary.gov
The Nixon Presidential Library and Museum is administered by the National Archives and Records Administration and hosts a

wealth of information on Nixon's life and presidency. Many of these documents, photographs, and recordings are available on the library's website.

Vietnam Veterans of America
8719 Colesville Road, Suite 100
Silver Spring, MD 20910
(301) 585-4000
Website: http://www.vva.org
Vietnam Veterans of America is a nonprofit organization that advocates for Vietnam veterans on health care, accounting for prisoners of war, exposure to toxins such as Agent Orange, and other issues.

Websites

Because of the changing nature of Internet links, Rosen Publishing has developed an online list of websites related to the subject of this book. This site is updated regularly. Please use this link to access the list:

http://www.rosenlinks.com/pppl/Nixon

For Further Reading

Archer, Jules. *Watergate: A Story of Richard Nixon and the Shocking 1972 Scandal.* New York, NY: Sky Pony Press, 2015.

Feinstein, Stephen. *The 1970s* (Decades of the 20th and 21st Centuries). New York, NY: Enslow Publishers, 2016.

Fremon, David K. *The Watergate Scandal in United States History.* Berkeley Heights, NJ: Enslow Publishers, 2014.

Greene, John Robert. *The Nixon–Ford Years* (Presidential Profiles). New York, NY: Facts on File, 2006.

Kamberg, Mary-Lane. *Affirmative Action: Legislating Equality and Opportunity* (A Celebration of the Civil Rights Movement). New York, NY: Rosen Publishing, 2015.

Kent, Deborah. *The Vietnam War: From Da Nang to Saigon* (The United States at War). Berkeley Heights, NJ: Enslow Publishers, 2011.

Killcoyne, Hope Lourie, ed. *Key Figures of the Vietnam War* (Biographies of War). New York, NY: Britannica Educational Publishing, 2016.

Robenalt, James. *January 1973: Watergate,* Roe v. Wade*, Vietnam, and the Month that Changed America Forever.* Chicago, IL: Chicago Review Press, 2015.

Schmitz, David F. *Richard Nixon and the Vietnam War: The End of the American Century.* Lanham, MD: Rowman & Littlefield, 2014.

Tudda, Chris. *A Cold War Turning Point: Nixon and China, 1969–1972.* Baton Rouge, LA: Louisiana State University Press, 2012.

Weiner, Tim. *One Man Against the World: The Tragedy of Richard Nixon.* New York, NY: Henry Holt and Company, 2015.

Wittekind, Erika. *The United States v. Nixon: The Watergate Scandal and Limits to US Presidential Power* (Landmark Supreme Court Cases). Minneapolis, MN : ABDO Publishing, 2013.

Woodward, Bob. *The Last of the President's Men.* New York, NY: Simon & Schuster, 2015.

Index